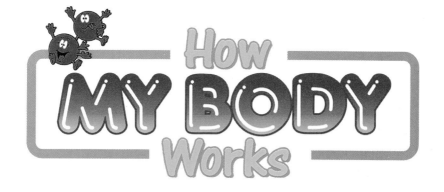

Immunisation

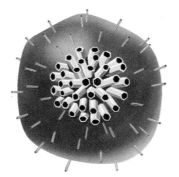

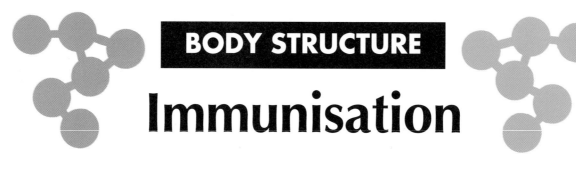

Immunisation

What is immunity?

Disease-spreading germs called **pathogens** are all around us. Every day our body has to fight against constant attacks by different dangerous bacteria and viruses. When the body is healthy its own defence system is capable of fighting these germs. But the body's defence army can only fight against micro-organisms that it has already seen and recognises from a past illness. In order to deal with unknown illnesses, special protective troops have to be used.

These defensive forces remain on guard against germs for the rest of our life. When the body's defence army is able to recognise and stop certain micro-organisms it is said to be **immune** against an illness. Immunity against an illness is the result of the body's defence army coming in contact with, and recognising, dangerous bacteria and viruses.

Nature provides protection against dangerous bacteria and viruses which try to attack us. Breast milk helps protect babies from illness, while older children develop immunity through actually having had an illness and producing antibodies.

The Professor directs the body's defence system. He and Metro, his lieutenant, work to protect your body. Globus and his team of red blood cells need protection as they travel the body delivering oxygen. So Captain Courageous, chief of the white corpuscles and his friends Ace and Corpo cruise around the body attacking their enemies Virulus, the virus and Toxicus, the bacterium.

VIRULUS

GLOBUS

PLASMUS

GLOBINA

CONTENTS

Different immune armies

Each type of animal has its own immune armies. Horses, for example, are immune to snake poison, while dogs are immune to scarlet fever, which is extremely dangerous for humans. Humans can become immune in two ways:

- **actively** – when someone has suffered from an illness and recovered from it. The special defence army that helped the body recover will stay in the blood for the rest of the person's life.
- **passively** – when a ready-made protective substance is put into the body, as in the case of unborn babies through their mother's blood, or new-born babies through breast milk.

Helping our body

We can help our body in its struggle to fight diseases in two ways:

● through **active immunisation** – a small amount of an illness is injected into the body. The germs are weakened or killed so that they do not actually give the body the illness. The defence army is able to recognise the attackers in the future and chase them away.

● through **passive immunisation** – a patient is given antibodies. These are proteins that can fight against a particular illness. Antibodies are usually taken from the blood of animals which have already overcome a particular illness.

Active immunisation is an important way to stop you catching a particular illness before the bacteria gets into your body. When a person is injected with a small amount of germs, they are said to be **vaccinated** against an illness. Hopefully they will not catch this illness.

Passive immunisation is a way of curing an illness. It is used for people who are already ill. Passive immunisation is used only when there is no time for active immunisation to become effective – if the body has already been invaded by bacteria. Passive immunisation is less effective and takes longer to work.

In the picture below, the Professor is taking blood from a horse to get antibodies.

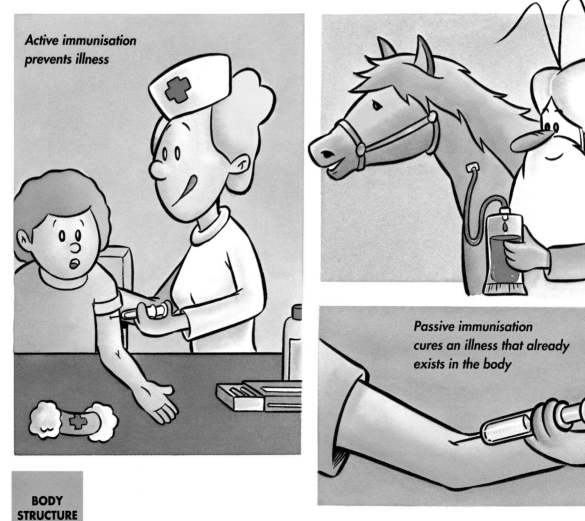

Active immunisation
prevents illness

Passive immunisation
cures an illness that already
exists in the body

DOES SMALLPOX STILL EXIST?

Smallpox was a disease that was very common until 1980, when it was declared extinct. For hundreds of years it was a very serious illness which killed large numbers of people and was one of the main causes for the high death rate in India. Smallpox spreads through direct contact with a person who already has the illness, or through breathing in germs.

People who suffer from smallpox have a very high temperature (40°Celsius) and red spots all over their bodies, which soon turn into small swellings called **pustules**. These spots are filled with pus.

As a result of smallpox vaccine (active immunisation) this illness has disappeared everywhere in the world. A few cases of smallpox were found in France in 1955, and at the beginning of 1962 there were even a few fatal cases of smallpox in England and Germany.

There is now a worldwide vaccination campaign and no new cases of smallpox have been recorded anywhere in the world since the 1970s. Today, scientists spend many hours trying to create vaccines that will fight other diseases from cancer and AIDS to hay fever.

The discovery of a vaccine

Vaccination against serious illnesses is extremely important. A vaccine gives a boost to the body's immune system. It makes the body sensitive to particular disease-causing bacteria. A vaccination can be taken by mouth or given by injection. We must take advantage of scientific achievements in modern medicine to make sure that serious illnesses such as smallpox, diphtheria, tetanus or polio no longer threaten us.

We owe the discovery of vaccination to Edward Jenner, an English doctor who lived in the 18th century. While reading a book about ancient Greek historians, he came across an interesting description about an epidemic in Athens, when a lot of people became ill at the same time.

The only people who could look after patients without any danger to themselves were people who had already had the illness but, for some unknown reason, had survived. They no longer needed to worry about becoming infected by the disease because they were now immune to it. Their immune system was able to recognise the virus and stop the disease-spreading germs from invading.

Jenner noticed that everyone who survived smallpox became immune to it. He then studied an illness very similar to smallpox which was found in cows, called cowpox. People who touched any cows suffering from cowpox became ill,

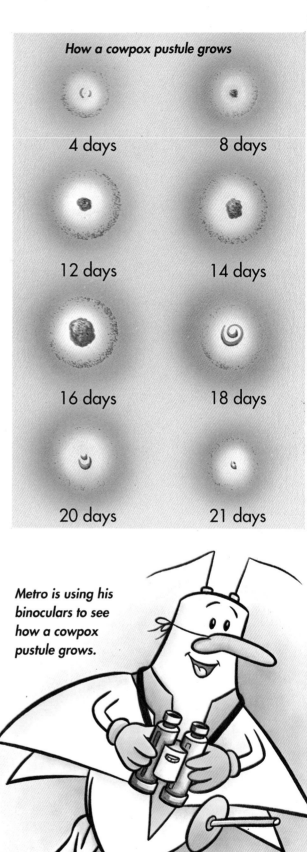

How a cowpox pustule grows

4 days   8 days

12 days   14 days

16 days   18 days

20 days   21 days

Metro is using his binoculars to see how a cowpox pustule grows.

but afterwards, they found that they were immune to smallpox. Jenner took a small amount of pus from a pustule on a person who had caught cowpox and injected this into a child who immediately became ill. Two months later, when the child had recovered, he injected the same child with pus from a smallpox pustule. This time the child did not become ill – he was now immune. Jenner had found that it was possible to develop an immunity against smallpox after having become infected with cowpox. It was many years later before the Frenchman Louis Pasteur was able to give a scientific explanation for Jenner's experiment. Pasteur realized that a vaccination with cowpox bacteria made the body produce antibodies which were able to fight against smallpox.

Antibodies remain in the blood for a long time but they sometimes need to be boosted. That is why you need to have vaccinations every ten years or so.

Edward Jenner

Edward Jenner made an important discovery – a person who has been infected with cowpox becomes immune to smallpox by making antibodies. He noticed that by injecting someone with a harmless illness, it was possible to become protected against a more serious form of the disease. The body could be encouraged to make antibodies to fight disease-spreading bacteria. He discovered the vaccination technology against smallpox and other illnesses and started a new science called immunology.

The Production Of Antibodies

Micro-organisms produce toxins ...

As soon as micro-organisms have entered the body, they are attacked by white blood cells. The body knows that germs are present because the micro-organisms release a substance which is an **antigen**, called a **toxin**. Toxins are dangerous proteins which harm the body and the body's defences are alerted. If the white blood cells cannot destroy the invaders on their own, the body's defence system then makes antibodies to fight the intruders. The antigen or toxin is the substance which the body recognises as the red-alert sign – antibodies are needed quickly.

... and lymphocytes make antibodies

The antibodies are made by white blood cells called **lymphocytes**. They do this when antigens or other bacterial toxins have alerted the body to their presence. The antigens or toxins will make the body ill if they are not dealt with quickly. Antibodies either stop toxins in their tracks, or repair the damage they have done. They do this by brewing up a mixture – the antigen-antibody reaction. This reaction takes place within part of the blood called **plasma**.

Just look at this lot! Micro-organisms love to gather between the cell tissues of a human body where they make horrible, poisonous substances called antigens or toxins. Here you can see a gang of disease-spreading bacteria brewing up a pot of toxins to damage the body. A swarm of small germs called pathogens is making its way up to the body organs where they can do the most damage: the bowel, the liver and the nerve centres.

Tonsils

Thymus gland

Lymph nodes

Spleen

Peyer's patches in the small intestine

Red bone marrow

Most white blood cells are made in bone marrow. When a baby is being formed, its bone marrow contains many cells ready to work in the body. The cells which will become lymphocytes move to the liver and spleen, where they form B-lymphocytes and to the thymus gland where they grow into T-lymphocytes. When B-lymphocytes fight against poisonous antigens they are helped by T-cells to produce antibodies.

This drawing shows the most important places in the body where white blood cells called lymphocytes are made and stored.

Where do antibodies come from?

The immune system in humans and more developed mammals is made up of several organs where lymphocytes, and antibodies, are processed and where the immune system workings are.

● **Red bone marrow** is a squishy substance found in sponge-like bone cells. In adults, it is found inside the flat bones as well as in the ends of long bones. Assorted shapes of white blood cells are made in the red bone marrow. Some of these become lymphocytes in the lymph nodes and in the lymphatic tissue of the spleen, liver and thymus gland. The changing stages of lymphocytes is shown in the illustrations below.

● The **thymus gland** distributes the white blood cells called T-lymphocytes until puberty and then it starts to get smaller and to hand the complete job over to red bone marrow.

● The **spleen** acts as a blood filter. It removes and destroys worn-out red blood cells and helps to fight infection.

● **Lymph nodes** filter the lymph and store up lots of lymphocytes. An inflammation of the lymph nodes is a sign that the body's defence system is fighting off harmful bacteria or viruses.

Most white blood cells are made in the bone marrow.

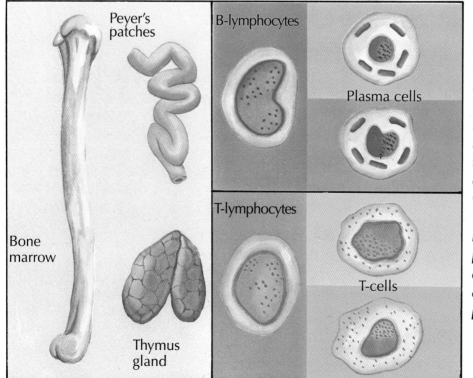

Bone marrow • Peyer's patches • Thymus gland • B-lymphocytes • Plasma cells • T-lymphocytes • T-cells

When a baby is being formed, its bone marrow contains many cells ready to work in the body. The cells which will become lymphocytes move to the Peyer's patches in the small intestine, where they form B-lymphocytes, and to the thymus gland, where they grow into T-lymphocytes. When lymphocytes fight against poisonous antigens, they are helped by plasma cells and T-cells to produce antibodies.

Inoculations for holidays

There are a number of things we can do to remain healthy when we go on holiday abroad. An inoculation protects a person against foreign germs. A small amount of bacteria from a foreign disease is injected into the body. If the body comes into contact with the disease, its defence system will recognise the bacteria and be able to defend itself. The World Health Organisation suggests which illnesses people should be inoculated against for each country. For instance, a traveller needs to be inoculated against typhoid, malaria and tuberculosis when they are going to India. As a result of these inoculations, travellers will be able to avoid infection, and they will not become carriers of these diseases. A carrier takes disease with them even though they may not appear to be ill. The table opposite lists the main dangerous illnesses and where they are found.

Illness	Areas in which the bacteria is common
Cholera	Mainly in Asia, and since 1970 also in Africa, south of the Sahara. The illness spreads mostly through bad drinking water and poor hygiene. Inoculation offers protection for only six months.
Yellow fever	Parts of Africa that are on the Equator, Central and South America. An inoculation for yellow fever is never given with one for polio because it will make you ill.
Smallpox	This disease appears to have been stopped in all countries of the world.
Typhoid and paratyphoid	In countries on the southern side of the equator and countries with poor standards of hygiene.
Rabies	In many countries throughout the world. Usually transmitted through an infected bite of a dog with the disease.
Tetanus or lockjaw	Can be caught anywhere. It is advisable to be inoculated every ten years. Having suffered from tetanus does not provide immunity.
Malaria	Mostly found in tropical countries. Travellers going to countries such as India and South America need to take protective medicine before, during and up to four weeks after the trip so that they are completely safe.
Hepatitis	In all countries. Hepatitis B is passed on through blood, particularly diseased blood given in blood transfusions. Hepititis A is passed on through bad food and water.
Polio	Tropical countries. Because of the serious threat of polio in the tropics, it is strongly recommended that all Europeans travelling to tropical countries are inoculated.

The antigen-antibody reaction

The body sets up a special defence mechanism which produces antibodies to fight against dangerous invaders. These invaders are called **antigens**.

Antibodies are found in the blood system after a person has already suffered from an illness. The body will have achieved victory over the antigens in the past, and will recognise them if they attack in the future. When the body's defence army recognises a certain illness and defends itself, the person is said to be **immune**.

Antibodies are like brave musketeers in the service of the human body. They defend their territory against invading armies of antigens. Antibodies fight bravely so that the body will remain healthy.

Antigens and antibodies are linked to each other. This means that an antibody produced to fight a diphtheria antigen will not be able to defend the body against smallpox antigens. Antibodies and antigens match each other like a key in a lock. It is possible for the correct antibody to cling on to an antigen and make it harmless. This formation is called the **antigen-antibody reaction**.

This reaction usually occurs between more than one antibody and one antigen. Large numbers of pairs cling to each other in small clumps and form a larger unit which is big enough to be seen with the eye. The glueing together of antibody and antigen pairs is called **agglutination**. It is very helpful to see large clumps of antibodies fighting antigens because doctors can see which illnesses a patient is immune to.

Also if a patient needs to have extra blood put into their body during an operation, doctors are able to match up suitable blood by recognising the antibodies. This means that the patient's defence army will not attack the good blood.

Each animal has its own set of genes. This means that each kind of animal can produce different antibodies which are made specially to help it survive. There are some animal diseases which humans do not suffer from and some diseases that animals cannot catch from humans. For instance, we cannot catch fowl pest which is a disease caught by chickens and chickens could never catch measles or polio.

Inoculations keep disease away

Illnesses are always dangerous and should be prevented where possible. Even if an illness will not kill you, it is not nice to feel unwell. One of the ways bacteria and viruses can be stopped is through inoculation. After being injected with a small amount of an illness, you may feel a bit unwell for a day or two. But it is all worth it, if the vaccine prevents you from getting a much more serious attack of a dangerous disease.

When an antigen is injected into the body the immune system starts to produce antibodies. These match the antigen and make it harmless. This is called a **primary reaction**. If the antigen enters the body again later, the body is able to make large numbers of antibodies in a short time with the help of its memory cells. This stage is known as a **secondary reaction**. It makes sure that the invading antigens are immediately destroyed so that the disease does not harm the body.

Poor little thing! He has got the measles. His parents are worried that his friends might catch the infection from him and so he is not allowed to go out to play and has to stay in bed. But one of his friends is allowed to come and visit him because she has already had measles and is now immune. When our patient is better, he too will be immune to measles because he has already successfully got rid of the invading germs.

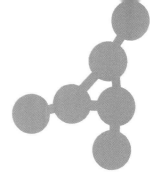

Dangerous Illnesses

Tetanus is very dangerous

Even a small cut can result in a horrible illness called **tetanus** or lockjaw. Tetanus germs can enter the body through a cut in the skin. Once it is inside the body, it attacks the nerves so they are no longer able to control the muscles.

When someone has caught tetanus their whole body slowly becomes paralysed. Their face and neck become stiff and then the stiffness spreads to the rest of the body.

If the patient is not treated, he could die because his breathing muscles become infected and do not work properly. Now you can see why it is so important to be inoculated and protected against this and all other dangerous illnesses.

Never neglect a cut. Always disinfect it, especially if it is deep or was caused by a rusty object or something in the garden. Tetanus is a horrible disease.

It is very important to make sure that you are inoculated against it. If you get a bad cut, go to the hospital or the doctor to find out if you need a booster.

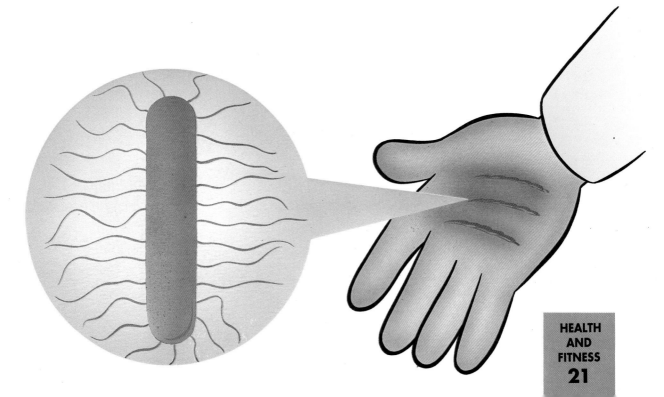

The invaders succeed

When disease-causing agents manage to beat the body's defence army, the antigens begin to damage the body. This means you have caught an illness. These are the stages of an illness:

● **Incubation period** – the time it takes for bacteria to make themselves at home somewhere in the body. They will begin to produce a lot of antigens or toxins. At this point, the patient will not know about the invaders because there are still no signs of the illness and so he will not feel ill – the illness is incubating. When the illness is incubating, the patient will still be seeing his friends and he might pass on the disease to other people. This is how epidemics start.

● **Illness** – when the body fights against microbes which have invaded it. The patient now has **symptoms**, signs of the illness, such as a high temperature, aches and pains.

● **Cure or recovery** – the period during which the patient is getting better. The patient is usually quite weak after an illness and the body's defences are low. The body needs rest and healthy food for a couple of days to make sure that the illness does not come back.

What are those greedy microbes in the top picture cooking in their big pot? It is the antigen brew. The disease is in the incubation phase. In the middle picture you can see a white blood cell being attacked by antigens. What a pest they are! The disease is in full swing. In the bottom picture, you can see our patient. The fight which took place in his body has left him very weak and tired.

When infection is greatest

Infections are dangerous things. When a disease is in the incubation stage we are unable to tell that it is in our body. It is possible to spread the illness to a lot of people as we don't know that we are ill. Germs that have a long incubation stage, for example, flu and glandular fever germs are most dangerous at this time. The danger of spreading other diseases is at its highest after the illness has started. This is true for measles, and chicken pox.

The table below shows when different illnesses are at their most infectious.

Illness	When it is most dangerous
Measles	It is easy to pass on the disease at the start of the illness but the danger decreases after the rash has appeared.
German measles	There is already a risk of infection two to four days before the rash appears.
Chicken pox	It is infectious from the day before the first blister appears until seven days after the disappearance of the last spot.
Mumps	It is most infectious when the glands and neck become swollen.
Whooping cough	Unless treated with antibiotics there is a possibility of infection until six weeks after the start of the illness. If the illness is treated with antibiotics there is no longer any risk of infection after seven days.
Scarlet fever	It is at its most infectious during the first days of the illness. Scarlet fever stops being infectious 24 hours after starting treatment with antibiotics.
Polio	It is infectious until paralysis begins.

Keeping healthy

Today, because of the discoveries of scientists we have many ways of preventing illnesses or curing them. By following these few simple steps we can keep ourselves clean and keep our environment hygienic.

● Kill germs and stop the spread of dangerous disease carriers – keep the kitchen clean and be careful when handling food. If you get a cut or graze, use disinfectant on it immediately.

● Clean up waste and rubbish. Make sure that it is not left lying around to rot because this encourages bacteria to grow – put waste into rubbish bins. Germs like dirty places!

● Make sure that the medicine cupboard is well stocked to deal quickly with an illness. Know who your local doctor is and where the nearest hospital with an emergency department is.

● Help the government keep our water and air clean by following environmentally friendly practices.

Here are three ways that provide a healthy environment. Reducing waste and correctly disposing of it, installing modern technical equipment in hospitals, using special purification plants for water and fighting dangerous disease carriers are all important.

Sadly, there are still many countries where there is not enough money, or suitable governmental organisation, to be able to provide these basic health standards. Some countries do not have a good medical service for everyone to use. There are many ways, through international charities, to help people in these countries.

ONCE IN A LIFETIME

Some diseases can be caught over and over again because they only make the body immune to invading micro-organisms for a short time. This is the case with flu, colds and tonsillitis. Many other serious diseases usually only need one course of inoculation for long-term protection against the invaders. These illnesses include:

- Diphtheria
- Measles
- Mumps

- Yellow fever
- Whooping cough
- Rabies

- German measles
- Chicken pox
- Tuberculosis

When you have had one of these illnesses or been inoculated against it, an invisible shield is formed. This protects you from the agents of that disease.

The Professor has had his measles inoculation and so the measles germs now just bounce off.

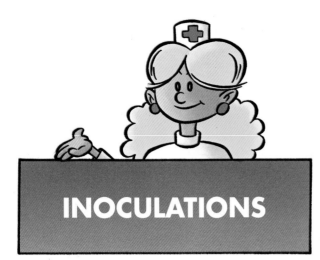

INOCULATIONS

Let's all keep healthy

I expect you have seen a children's inoculation chart. For some diseases it is necessary to be inoculated several times during your life because complete immunity is only achieved after a first inoculation followed by one or more repeat injections called **boosters**. That is why you must never miss any of the dates.

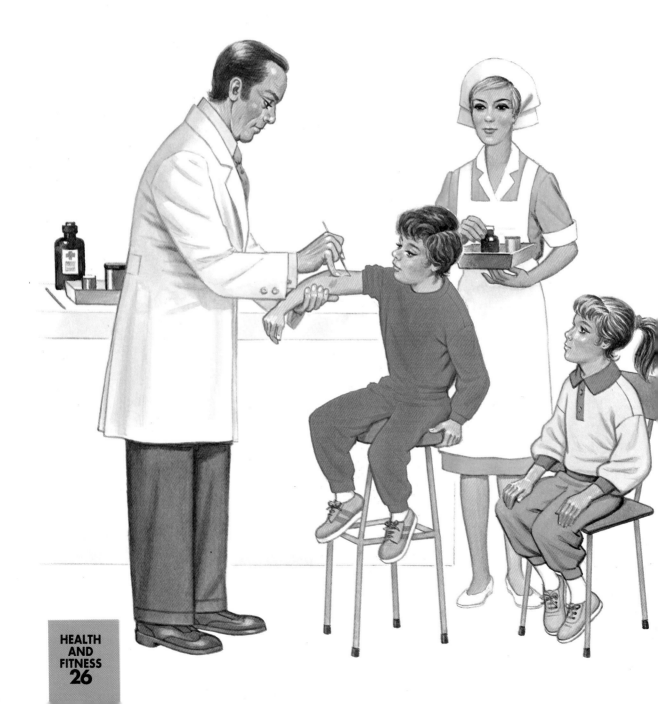

Age	Inoculation	Note
3 months	Diphtheria, tetanus, polio, whooping cough	DTP inoculation
4/5 months	Second DTP	Repeat inoculation
15/24 months	DTP Measles, mumps, rubella	Repeat inoculation Known as MMR
5/7 years	Diphtheria, tetanus and tuberculosis	BCG inoculation
12/15 years	MMR	If it has not been done before

Inoculation against certain diseases seems quite normal to children today. But your grandparents will tell you that there were very few inoculations when they were children. People used to think that inoculations were actually dangerous, and doctors had to work hard to persuade parents to have their children treated. Now it is agreed that unless you have particular medical problems in your family it is best for all children to have all the inoculations.

KEY WORDS

Agglutination – clumping together of cells in the presence of antibodies.

Antibodies – anti-toxins produced in the blood plasma as a reaction to the invasion of antigens in the body.

Antigen – foreign protein (bacteria) which brings about the production of antibodies.

Blood transfusion – giving blood from a healthy person to a sick person.

Fowl pest – devastating epidemic disease which mainly affects chickens. Humans are immune to it.

Hepatitis – infection of the liver.

Immune – resistant to disease.

Immunology – the science which studies the subject of immunity.

Incubation – the period between infection and the appearance of symptoms of an illness.

Injection – putting a medicinal substance into the body with a needle.

Oral – taking something by mouth. An oral vaccination is not injected but is swallowed, as in the case of polio vaccine.

Third World – political term to describe economically under-developed countries (Asia, Africa and Latin America), as opposed to the industrial countries of the West.

Toxin – poisonous substance produced by bacteria.

Waste disposal – the removal of waste and making it harmless.

WHO – World Health Organisation; an international organisation of the United Nations dealing with all aspects of health matters in every country in the world. The WHO is the highest international body for matters concerning public health.

HOW MY BODY WORKS

HOW MY BODY WORKS is an educational series that builds into a complete encyclopedia of the human body. Each volume introduces and explains one of its mysteries.

In Part 24 of How My Body Works, you've discovered the immunisation system and how vaccines work.

PART 25 looks at hormones and how they are different for men and women.

READ ALL ABOUT:
● **Chemicals called hormones**, that rush around the body sending messages.
● **The growth hormone** that makes sure people are the right size.
● **How animals use hormones to communicate** and find out who is a friend and who isn't.

Albert Barillé, (pictured left) is the author of this fascinating series of books. The human body is a series of complex systems and mechanisms, so to make it easier for you to understand how the body works, Barillé created The Professor, Captain Courageous, Globus, Toxicus and Virulus, plus many other colourful cartoon characters, to show you around. The Professor and his friends guide you through the body, explaining how it works in a clear and simple way that makes it fun.

TEST YOUR KNOWLEDGE

The Immunisation Quiz

1. What are disease-spreading germs called?
a) antigens
b) pathogens
c) germers

2. When is the body immune?
a) when its defence army recognises and stops invading germs
b) when it recognises invaders but doesn't stop them
c) when it doesn't recognise invading bacteria

3. What is passive immunisation?
a) a harmless disease
b) when a patient is given antibodies
c) an inoculation that makes you go to sleep

4. What are pustules filled with?
a) slime
b) healing liquid
c) pus

5. How does a vaccine work?
a) it gives a boost to the body's immune system
b) it fights invading micro-organisms
c) it makes the blood red

6. What is a toxin?
a) a substance released by micro-organisms
b) a drink
c) polluted waste

7. Where are lymphocytes made?
a) in bone marrow
b) in the Peyer's patches
c) in the spleen

8. What makes antibodies?
a) tonsils
b) white blood cells
c) plasma

9. Where is malaria found?
a) in South America
b) in tropical countries
c) in France

10. How many stages does an illness have?
a) three
b) one
c) it depends on the illness

11. Where do germs like living?
a) in dirty places
b) in sick people
c) where they can't be found

12. How can you keep healthy?
a) clean up waste and rubbish
b) make sure that the medicine cupboard is well stocked
c) keep the kitchen clean

ANSWERS to the **'How My Body Works'** Immunisation Quiz in issue 25.

Answers to issue 23:
1 (a), 2 (c), 3 (b), 4 (a & b), 5 (b), 6 (b), 7 (b), 8 (a & b), 9 (b), 10 (a), 11 (a)

Note: Issue 16 of How My Body Works contained a reference to children taking aspirin for toothache. We would like to point out that only children over 12 should, in fact, take aspirin. Parents with children under this age should seek medical advice for the best form of pain relief.

Published by
ORBIS PUBLISHING,
Griffin House,
161 Hammersmith Road,
London W6 8SD

BACK ISSUES
Back issues can be obtained by placing an order with your newsagent or, in case of difficulty, from our back numbers department. All cheques/postal orders should be made payable to Orbis Publishing Ltd.

BACK ISSUE CHARGES
Volume 1:
UK: 99p plus £1.00 p&p;
Eire: IR£0.99 plus £1.00 p&p
Thereafter:
UK: £2.99 plus 50p p&p;
Eire: IR£3.50 plus 50p p&p

ADDRESS FOR BACK ISSUES:
Orbis Publishing Ltd, Unit 10, Wheel Lane Business Park, Wheel Lane, Westfield, Hastings, East Sussex, TN35 4SG. Tel: 0424 755755

BACK ISSUES OVERSEAS
Please place requests for copies of back issues with your newsagent or, in case of difficulty, please write to the relevant address given:

Australia
Gordon and Gotch Ltd, PO Box 290, Burwood VIC 3125 (Enclose cover price plus $1 p&h per issue)

New Zealand
Gordon and Gotch (NZ) Ltd, PO Box 584, Auckland.

Malta, Singapore & South Africa Back numbers are available at LM1.50 from your newsagent.

© Procidis Albert Barillé
© 1993 Orbis Publishing Ltd, London
N24 93 08 05
Printed in Italy
by Officine Grafiche
De Agostini, Novara